» Simple Guides

THERAVADA
BUDDHISM

» Simple Guides

THERAVADA BUDDHISM

Diana & Richard St Ruth

Published in Great Britain by
Simple Guides, an imprint of Bravo Ltd
59 Hutton Grove, London N12 8DS
www.kuperard.co.uk
Enquiries: office@kuperard.co.uk

First published 1998 by Global Books Ltd.
This edition published 2007

ISBN 978 1 85733 434 0

British Library Cataloguing in Publication Data
A CIP catalogue entry for this book
is available from the British Library

Printed in Malaysia

Cover image: Buddha images, Ayutthaya. *istockphoto/Jeremy Edwards*
Drawings by Irene Sanderson

About the Authors

BOTH THE AUTHORS were born in 1943, Richard in London, Diana in Leicester, and both developed an interest in Buddhism during their teens. They were married in 1969. In 1983 they founded the Buddhist Publishing Group, and in 1989 started the magazine *Buddhism Now*, of which they are joint editors. They also organize annual Buddhist summer schools. Other titles by the authors include: *An Introduction to Buddhism*, BPG, 1988; *Zen Graffiti*, BPG 1991; *Experience Beyond Thinking: A Guide to Buddhist Meditation*, BPG, 1993; *The Little Book of Buddhist Wisdom*, Element, 1997; *Sitting: A Guide to Buddhist Meditation*, Penguin, 1998; and in the Simple Guide series, *Zen Buddhism*.

We would like to express our grateful thanks to Don E. Whitbread for his helpful comments on the manuscript.

⟩ Contents

List of Illustrations

⌃ *Buddha in teaching pose.* © *Photo: Richard St Ruth*

Theravada is the Buddhism of Sri Lanka, Thailand, Myanmar (Burma), Laos and other Southeast Asian countries.

It is the oldest school of Buddhism that exists today, and the texts which have been preserved, known as the Pali Canon, are believed to contain some of the original teachings of the Buddha. Theravada means Way of the Elders. It is also known as the Southern School of Buddhism.

In general, Theravada is a devotional, gentle form of Buddhism, with emphasis on generosity. Its teachings are based upon tolerance, mindfulness, morality and insight which lead to wisdom, compassion, and liberation from suffering. Its form is centred upon the monastic system, a system which interacts closely with the lay community.

The interest that Theravada has stimulated in the West is twofold – (i) in the cultural and monastic traditions which have evolved over the centuries and are being practised to this day, and (ii) discovering the wisdom which lies within its teachings and attempting to apply them in a modern, Western context.

DIANA AND RICHARD ST RUTH
Sandwell, Devon.

⊙ *Bodhi Leaf from a descendant of the tree under which the Buddha became enlightened*

Chapter 1

History

Roots in India

Buddhism has its roots and origins in India, a land which has a long and rich history of religion and culture going back to ancient times.

During the thirteenth century BCE the Indo-Iranians (Aryans), a branch of the Indo-Europeans, invaded northwest India. As a result, the Indo-Iranian holy texts, the *Vedas* (compiled between the fifteenth and the sixth centuries BCE) and the Vedic tradition were gradually assimilated into the older beliefs of the Indian people. Between the sixth and seventh centuries BCE this combination of beliefs gradually developed into what became known as Brahmanism.

It was in this atmosphere of strong cultural traditions and religious beliefs, more than 2,500 years ago, that Siddhattha (the man who was to become the Buddha) was born and embarked upon his spiritual career.

⊙ *The Stupa, Sanchi, Madhya Pradesh, India*

The Oldest School of Buddhism

Though its beginnings are obscure, Theravada is believed to be one of the very oldest schools of Buddhism.

In approximately 483 BCE, not long after the Buddha's death, an important meeting took place among his followers; this became known as the

First Council. It is said that at this First Council, one of the Buddha's chief disciples, Ananda, repeated all he could remember of the teachings. Ananda's recollections were then learned by rote by many of those present, and these people subsequently passed on their recollections word-for-word to others. This method then became the accepted way of preserving the Buddha's teachings, and what evolved were the repetitive chants that can still be heard today in Buddhist monasteries and temples. It was a way of preserving the teachings; and it probably also had the effect of systematizing them at that time.

Buddhist texts usually open with the words 'Thus have I heard . . .' This reflects the fact that they are being recounted and that what follows are not necessarily the actual words of the Buddha.

Schisms in the Order

During the first hundred years after the demise of the Buddha, some disciples began to specialize in studying the discourses of the Buddha (the *suttas*), and others made a study of the rules of behaviour (the *vinaya*) said to have been devised by the Buddha. This specialization led to debate, and these debates, it is thought, led, to the schisms which followed.

A hundred years later, in about 340 BCE, a Second Council was called. It was at this time that a very important split took place. This resulted in what basically became two factions known as the Great Sangha (the Mahasanghikas), and the Sthaviras, meaning 'the Elders'. This division was primarily the result of a dispute about the qualities needed for one to become a Holy One, an *Arahant*.

During the following century various other schisms took place on the question of doctrine, the rules of the Buddhist order, and a metaphysical view of the Buddha.

The Sthaviras divided into many schools. Convention has it that there were eighteen groups. The texts and commentaries, however, mention more. The Indian Sanskrit term 'Sthavira' meaning 'Elder' became the Pali word 'Theravada', 'the Way of the Elders', in the Southeast Asian countries which subsequently adopted and preserved the teachings.

In the eleventh century, these teachings left India, but the Theravada tradition that exists today evolved from these early Indian beginnings.

⌃ Gold-lacquered Buddha. Burmese 18th – 19th c.
(The Bhuddist Society, London.) © Photo: Diana St Ruth

Hinayana (the Small Vehicle)

The other major faction, the Mahasanghikas, eventually became known as Mahayanists – Great Vehicle Buddhists*. The Mahayanists began to refer to the Theravadans as Hinayanists – Small Vehicle Buddhists. The comparison was meant as a derogatory term to point out the 'small mindedness' of the Theravadans who were working for their own salvation only, while the Mahayanists were working for the liberation of everyone. It was saying that the Great Vehicle will carry many to liberation, while the Small Vehicle will carry but one. This understanding was unwittingly adopted by early Western scholars who then set a pattern in translation which others followed.

A counter claim also emerged through the translations of the Theravada writings, and stated that the Theravada was the 'original teaching', and therefore the pure, unadulterated, orthodox version.

These terms and claims were, basically, an ancient sectarian argument brought into the modern age. They were out of context and referred to groups that existed over two thousand years

* Originally, the term 'Mahasanghikas' (Great Sangha) probably referred to the size of the group. They were the majority.

ago. These errors in translation and interpretation are now gradually being ironed out, but there are still many references to Hinayana, meaning Theravada, to be found in Buddhist works.

Development of the Schools

Buddhist history has been one of constant development. Schools, such as the Theravada, have gone through long processes of change and transformation, and none that exist today should be regarded as an exact replica of any group in existence at the time of the Buddha.

The great Councils were momentous occasions, but analysis and debate were ongoing processes throughout the ages which affected gradual change. The early Buddhist communities (*sangha*) were small groups of practising ascetics. The Buddha would teach his followers and then urge them to go and meditate in forests and caves. Naturally, when these people came together to discuss their experiences, interpretations would differ. What today would seem to be great splits in these early groups, therefore, may merely have been issues of debate, just people putting their own interpretations on their insights. During the time of the great Buddhist university at Nalanda which flourished over a thousand years after these early days, for example, monks of different persuasions lived and studied together.

During this process of change and debate, the rules of the Buddhist community remained fairly constant amongst all traditions. There was never much discussion about how a Buddhist should live; controversy centred mainly upon the consequences of the Buddhist way of life; these were mere philosophical debates.

Early Years

Very little is actually known of Theravada Buddhism as it existed in India, of course, all those centuries ago, although it is thought to have been widespread in the northern areas. The first recorded accounts of it are from the time of the Indian Emperor Ashoka (274–236 BCE) who sent his son, Mahinda, to Sri Lanka as a missionary.

In Sri Lanka, Theravada was established and became the state religion. This was in about 250 BCE. From there it moved on to Thailand in approximately 720 CE, though it could have first appeared there much earlier, and came into

Myanmar (Burma) in about 1100 CE, and then on to various other countries in Southeast Asia. In the nineteenth century Theravada, with other forms of Buddhism, came to the West, where today it has begun to take root.

Strangely, Buddhism began to die out in India around 1200 CE and is now virtually extinct in its land of origin.

The Pali Language

The ancient texts of the Theravada were written in Pali. This, like its closely related cousin, Sanskrit, of the Mahayana school, is a dead language, only to be heard these days in the Buddhist temples being chanted by monks. One or two Pali words, however, have found their way into the modern languages, as no appropriate translations can be found. In the West, though, the Sanskrit versions are generally used. We see *nirvana* (Sanskrit), for example, rather than the Pali equivalent *nibbana*; *dharma* (Sanskrit) rather than *dhamma* (Pali); *karma* (Sanskrit) rather than *kamma* (Pali), and so on. (See Glossary.)

Note: CE = Common Era, i.e. AD – Anno Domini
     BCE = Before the Common Era

⌄ Wat Prasingh, Chiangmai, Thailand

Chapter 2

The Life of the Buddha

Siddhattha

Siddhattha Gotama, approximately 563–483 BCE;* is the man who became the Buddha, the Fully Enlightened One. The legends surrounding his life are varied, but they have a common theme.

Siddhattha was born of a noble or royal family in Kapilavatthu on the borders of present-day Nepal and India. The Gotamas were a branch of the Sakya clan.

His mother, Maya, gave birth to him in a grove in Lumbini. She died seven days later and his aunt, Prajapati, took over as foster mother. The family were of the warrior (*khattiya*) caste.

A holy man saw the baby and predicted it would have a choice in later life of becoming either a great monarch or a great spiritual leader. Siddhattha's father, Suddhodana, had no doubts in his mind what he wanted his son to be – a great monarch – and he instituted a life of luxury and

⊘ *The Great Departure.*
Burmese boy re-enacts the
scene as he leaves the family
to enter the monastry as a
novice monk

ease for the boy, keeping him from the dark side
of existence with all its disappointments and
suffering, fearing that if Siddhattha's compassion
were aroused, he would be tempted into a
religious career. And so Siddhattha saw nothing
of old age, sickness and death.

* Some Buddhists, especially in Japan, believe that the Buddha lived
from 448–368 BCE

Old Age

In spite of the carefully orchestrated days, however, and his father's attempts to fill his every moment with light-hearted extravagances, Siddhattha was unhappy and would reflect deeply on the nature of existence.

As the years passed, he became curious about what lay beyond the palace gates, those gates which were always firmly shut and guarded. He was never allowed to roam freely beyond the confines of the palaces. Whenever he went anywhere it was always formally, with a huge entourage and lots of pomp and circumstance. Suddenly, he felt like a prisoner and he wondered, 'What is it like out there? How do other people live?' He knew what it was like when things were organized for him, when the streets were lined with cheering crowds and festooned with colourful flags and banners, but what was it like to mix with the ordinary people on an ordinary day, when they did not know who he was? His curiosity grew.

Siddhattha knew his father would never agree to his wandering unofficially and unannounced, and so he plotted with his charioteer to slip by the palace guards. They drove unseen one day through the gates, out and along the tracks leading to town. There they joined the crowds, unnoticed in their ordinary garb, and mingled freely with the people.

Siddhattha was fascinated by all that he saw — everyone going about their business, groups chatting, lively trading on the roadside. And then he noticed something strange – was it a man? He could not be sure. It seemed to be like a man, but it was all bent up, incredibly wrinkled, covered in rags, and begging. Siddhattha asked the charioteer: 'What kind of being is this? Why does he look so strange? What's wrong with him?'

'This is simply an old man,' said the charioteer, 'We all get old.' Siddhattha was taken aback, shocked even. Would he and his family get old? Does everyone become decrepit like that man? Shaken by this revelation, Siddhattha asked to be taken home where he contemplated that man and old age.

Sickness and Death

Siddhattha's curiosity was roused even more now, and he made a second trip with his faithful charioteer to the nearby town where people lived so differently. This time, they happened to come across a sick man, writhing in agony and covered in sores. Turning to his charioteer once more for an explanation, he was told, 'This is a sick man. Sickness comes in many forms to all of us in time, before we die.' Wistfully, the prince turned away, but just in time to see a funeral procession passing by, and a dead body being transported to the pyre. 'And this?'

'This is death,' said the charioteer, 'and these are the mourners.'

Sickness? Death? Once again, a saddened and pensive prince returned to the palace, disturbed by the things he did not expect to see.

Leaving Home

Siddhattha had become deeply aware that all beings become old, get sick and die. The legend is that this was the first time he encountered such things in life, but perhaps it was that this was the first time he had become completely conscious of them, and it brought on a lot of questioning: 'What was life all about if it ends like this?' He could not stop thinking about it and became completely unsettled, his own luxurious way of life losing all of its meaning and charm.

Suddenly, the most important thing in the world for him was to know the reasons for life's miseries – why people suffered in poverty and sickness, why all beings were born, apparently just to die. Deep within himself he felt the need, the compulsion, to find out. 'Surely,' he told himself, 'someone must know the truth of all this – the holy men, perhaps?'

Despite the pleas of his wife and his father, and despite the fact that he had a young son, Rahula, Siddhattha left home in search of truth and enlightenment. He was twenty-nine.

Searching for Truth

At first, he lived in the way that other holy men lived in those days, dressed in rags and begging food, sometimes subsisting on whatever wild fruits and nuts could be found in the forest, sometimes not eating at all. He learned how to be an ascetic, how to meditate, how to perform rites and rituals.

Six years passed, six austere years, under first one guru and then another – meditating, searching passionately for truth, undertaking severe ascetic practices which left him weak and near to death. It is said that at the culmination of these practices he was eating just one grain of rice a day and slowly starving to death. Then, as he became aware that his life-energy was ebbing away, he suddenly realized the futility of what he was doing. He began to take stock of himself and contemplated the past few years. What progress had he made? What had he accomplished by performing religious rites and rituals, by contemplating philosophical views, by the self-infliction of physical pain? None of these things had led to truth. He realized that to kill the senses was no better than to overindulge them, that ascetic practices were pointless, and that the gurus he had met were not fully enlightened. Suddenly, he knew what he must do and became resolute.

The Cool of a Tree

He ate a meal of rice – the first really nourishing meal he had had for a long time. And then, revitalized and inspired, he sought the cool of a tree. Now he was determined and completely ready to turn within himself, to seek for the answers there, leaving aside all the practices and methods he had learned and had become reliant upon. Touching the earth with his hand, he called upon it to bear witness, determining never again to rise from that spot until complete enlightenment had been realized.

Enlightenment

Siddhattha's mind, having grown tired of beliefs, views and opinions, became tranquil, yet alert. He saw the fears and temptations within himself, and recognized them as the nature of evil. He noticed that that recognition alone broke their spell. He turned away from all the fears and temptations that were coming up in his mind, and they faded away.

He then contemplated the nature of suffering and the truth of desire. He realized that desire brought dissatisfaction and sorrow, and that there was no anguish without desire. All forms of wanting came to an end within him, even wanting truth; it all died away, and with it all dissatisfaction and suffering came to a complete stop.

Then came the realization that the thinking mind and the physical body are constantly changing, utterly impermanent, that there is nothing solid and fixed in either of them. He saw that it was his attachment to particular thoughts and specific forms which gave rise to the idea of 'self', 'me', believing that he owned a mind and owned a body, and he began to realize that birth, decay and death were the province of thoughts and forms only, and were not of the true nature of what he was.

Then he woke up to the unborn, the uncreated, the unmade, out of which came all that is born, created, and made. The truth dawned on him, and all manner of mysteries unfolded. He knew then he was fully awakened, Buddha.

The First Teaching

After his enlightenment, Siddhattha deliberated on whether to teach others. He was not at all sure it was possible to convey what he had realized, something so subtle and beyond words. Could he make it understandable through language, through concepts, through explanations? Despite a resistance to do so, he knew he must try, and he decided to look for the companions who had left him at the abandonment of his ascetic practices.

He found them at the Deer Park in Sarnath near Benares, and it was to these five that Siddhattha Gotama, now the Buddha, gave his first sermon. This, one might say, was where the teaching of Buddhism began.

The Buddha taught for the next forty-five years until he left this life at the age of eighty.

❯❯ The Word 'Buddha'

The word 'buddha' is not a proper name; it is a Pali word meaning 'awakened'. Siddhattha *became* the Buddha, the Awakened One, the Fully Enlightened One, in the same way that Jesus *became* Christ.

The word 'buddha', then, is a generic term and can refer to any being or state of being which is awakened, but references to 'the Buddha' usually imply Siddhattha, the man who became the Buddha. He was also called Gotama Buddha, Gotama being his family name.

When referring to himself, the Buddha used the term 'Tathagata' which means 'thus come', 'just being here and now, spontaneously, without a personal identity'.

Chapter 3

Aims &
Beliefs

The Transcendence of Suffering

The aim of Buddhism is to awaken to truth, to tread the path of enlightenment, instead of the path of delusion. One does not *become* enlightened; one lives in freedom from delusion and in harmony with wisdom and compassion. This is a living truth, not something that one attains as an attribute.

There may seem to be an emphasis in Buddhism on suffering, and it is sometimes criticized as being a pessimistic religion. The emphasis, however, is really upon the truth of suffering and its cessation. The idea is to own up to one's own fears, anxieties, irritations and disappointments in life – which can be quite daunting – and then to transcend and find deliverance from them. Recognition is, in itself, the way of transcendence. Sometimes this can be a single act – the recognition of suffering and the transcending of it may occur simultaneously.

Know for Yourself

Enlightenment is a way of life which can be experienced by anyone. There are seven characteristics by which it can be known.

Seven Marks of Enlightenment

Mindfulness
Investigation
Energy
Joyous zest
Tranquillity
Concentration
Equanimity

Beliefs, views and opinions, are not ⊙ *Lotus flower* characteristics of enlightenment; they are what hinder it. Buddhists are advised to see that beliefs are not truths in themselves. When looked into,

what starts out as a belief may be found to be true
or false. If false, then there are no grounds for
believing in it any longer, and if true, then it is no
longer a belief.

When something is experienced in one's life, it
is known for what it is. That is where the difference
lies between delusion and enlightenment. The
passage opposite is taken from a well-known text
used to illustrate this essential Buddhist teaching.

⊙ *Buddha images, Wat Yai Chai Mongkol, Ayuttaya, Thailand*

❯❯ The Kalama Sutta

The Buddha was once in a town called Kalama, where he was asked, 'What is the best way of knowing if a religious teaching is true or not?' To which the Buddha replied, 'Do not be swayed by tradition, nor by scripture, nor by established principles. Do not believe a teaching just because you have heard it many times, or because you believe it to be true, or because you have surmised or reasoned that it is true. Nor should you base the truth upon someone else's seeming ability or attainment, nor out of respect for that person if he or she is your teacher.

'Kalamas, when you know for yourselves that a certain action of body, speech or mind is unskilful, blameworthy, unwise, then abandon that action.

'When you know for yourselves that a certain action of body, speech or mind is skilful, without blame, and is the wise thing to do, then cultivate it, practise it, abide in that way of life.

'Kalamas, see for yourselves whether or not greed, hatred or self-centred actions lead to misery. If they do, then abandon them.

'See for yourselves, Kalamas, whether or not non-attachment, compassion and kindness lead to happiness for both yourselves and for others. If they do, then practise them, do not abandon them, base your way of life on them, and you will soon know the truth.'

From the *Anguttara-Nikaya*

Trust

Knowing the truth is an essential theme of the
Buddha's teaching; knowing it for oneself. This
does not mean beliefs are to be crushed, but simply
to be recognized as beliefs rather than as solid
truths, things known.

Trust, on the other hand, is entirely different.
Trust, or faith, in what one is doing, is essential.
Otherwise, one would not even begin to tread the
path. But trust is not fixed or blind or based on
conditioning; it is an openness to the possibility
that one is on the right road.

Blind faith is the part of the mind that the
Buddha's teaching aims to throw light on, that
unquestioning blindness which takes things for
granted. If one blindly follows without question, the
mind can never wake up to the way things are.
This waking up is one's own responsibility and the
ultimate goal of Buddhism.

⊘ *The spectacular detail and ornamentation of the doorway to the Temple of the Emerald Buddha, Bangkok*

Chapter 4

Who can be a Buddhist?

Anyone can be a Buddhist; it is not conditional upon one's birth into a particular family, culture, or tradition, nor is it dependent upon signing on the dotted line.

The only prerequisite to regarding oneself a Buddhist is the wish to turn towards awakening as a refuge rather than towards ignorance, the wish to turn towards truth as a refuge, the wish to keep company with others who have similar aspirations as a refuge, and of keeping five precepts. These are called *The Three Refuges*.

The five precepts, the *panca-sila*, are considered to be the minimum standard needed to form the basis of a decent life for oneself and others. It is traditionally chanted three times and, together with a commitment to awakening, can be used as a way of formally declaring oneself a Buddhist. Buddhist temples ring out daily with the sound of these commitments:

⌄ *Buddhist priest in a Thai temple*

The Three Refuges
Buddham saranam gacchami
Dhammam saranam gacchami
Sangham saranam gacchami

I go to the Buddha for refuge
I go to the Dhamma for refuge
I go to the Sangha for refuge

These lines are chanted three times.

⊙ *Buddhapadipa Temple, Wimbledon, London*
© *Photo: Richard St Ruth*

The Five Precepts

1. *Panatipata veramani-sikkhapadam samadiyami.*
   I undertake to observe the precept to abstain from killing living beings.

2. *Adinnadana veramani-sikkhapadam samadiyami.*
   I undertake to observe the precept to abstain from taking things not given.

3. *Kamesu micchacara veramani-sikkhapadam samadiyami.*
   I undertake to observe the precept to abstain from sexual misconduct.

4. *Musavada veramani-sikkhapadam samadiyami.*
   I undertake to observe the precept to abstain from false speech.

5. *Surameraya-majja-pamadatthana veramani-sikkhapadam samadiyami.*
   I undertake to observe the precept to abstain from intoxicating drinks and drugs causing heedlessness.

If one were unwilling to at least try to keep these moral precepts or to aspire towards awakening, then one could not really call oneself a Buddhist, not in the spiritual sense, that is. The precepts are, of course, interpreted in a multitude of ways and many people take the fifth one, for example, to mean it is okay to have an occasional glass of wine, but not to get drunk, or not to get drunk too often, anyway. Also, of course, those born into Buddhist families will automatically regard themselves as Buddhists whatever they do, much the same as most people do in other religions.

How Buddhists Think of Themselves

Many, especially in the East, regard their spiritual roles as supporters of the *sangha*, the order of monks, believing that there is nothing more important in life than to provide for monks to live and practise (the feeling is not the same towards nuns who are of a lower status). The belief is that generosity towards monks will bring good fortune in the future, or in future lives. In consequence, monks are sometimes incredibly well catered for.

It is unfortunate that prejudice against women is still prevalent in Eastern countries where it is often said that women cannot become enlightened in this life, that the best they can do is live decently and hope to be born a man next time. This, of course, was not the teaching of the Buddha who regarded men and women equally. Women in the

West are ignoring these old prejudices, as they are also beginning to do so more and more in the East.

Many Buddhists think of themselves purely as followers of the Buddha's teaching, as meditators trying to adhere to particular practices during their normal, everyday lives. This is true of Buddhists around the globe.

Others think of themselves as simple wayfarers, rather than as practitioners of a religion – seekers who do not label themselves as anything. The Buddha taught, in fact, that the teaching is to be used as a tool, a device, not something to be carried around on one's back as a burden. This is a point he puts across most graphically in his simile of the Raft.

The Simile of the Raft

'I shall explain,' he said to his monks, 'how the teaching (*dhamma*) is similar to a raft.

'Suppose someone is on a journey and comes to a great expanse of water. The near side is dangerous and frightening, and the further side is safe. Unfortunately, there is no means of crossing the water – no boat or bridge. So this person thinks: "I could collect some grass, twigs, branches, and leaves, and bind them together to make a raft. It would then be possible, by making an effort with my hands and feet, to use such a raft to get safely to the far shore."

'That person then makes the raft and goes across. Now, having arrived at the other shore, he might then think, "This raft has been very helpful to me. I'll hoist it onto my shoulders and go on my way with it." What do you think? Would that person be doing the right thing?'

'No, venerable sir,' answered the monks.

'On the other hand, that person might think, "This raft has been very helpful to me, but now I'll haul it onto the dry land or set it adrift in the water, and then go on my way." This, indeed, would be the right thing to do with that raft.

'The *dhamma* is similar to a raft. It is for crossing over to the other shore, not for carrying about and keeping. When you know that the teaching is similar to a raft, you should abandon even good states, let alone bad ones.'

A characteristic of Buddhism is that it is a religion which is not a religion. The teachings are to be used and then put down, otherwise there will be no freedom to go on. It would be regarded as foolish, for example, to hold the view that one is 'a Buddhist' and 'doing Buddhism', and of being separate and different from others who happen to follow other religions. There would be no freedom in having that kind of view. It would also be an indication that one was attached to dogma, which would be quite against the spirit of the Buddha's teachings.

Chapter 5

Sacred Texts & Basic Teachings

Legend has it that in about 100 BCE war and famine left the Buddhist order in Sri Lanka in danger of coming to an end. In consequence, the teaching, having been transmitted orally up to that time, was also in danger of being lost. It was at this time that the texts and commentaries were committed to writing – the texts in Pali and the commentaries in Sri Lankan.

The complete work became known as the *Tipitaka*, The Three Baskets, which is referred to in the West as The Pali Canon. This large work is in three parts:

- The *Vinaya-pitaka* – the origins of the *sangha* and the rules of discipline for monks and nuns,
- The *Sutta-pitaka* – the discourses of the Buddha and his disciples,
- The *Abhidhamma-pitaka* – Buddhist psychology and philosophy.

In the fifth century, Buddhagosha, (an Indian monk) compiled and edited the Pali Canon in Sri Lanka. This is what exists today. It is not known what the original Canon was really like.

⊙ *Wheel representing the eightfold path of the Buddha's teaching*

Three Signs of Being

Being a religion of personal experience, Buddhism
has developed a strong analytical side. Existence is
examined from every angle. In fact, in the early part
of the twentieth century it was this analytical
aspect of Buddhism which drew many people's
attention to it in the West. Buddhism was being
favourably compared to new discoveries in the
scientific and psychoanalytical worlds.

To a certain extent, this was a correct
assessment because this is the way Buddhism is,
though a closer look will reveal a subjective, non-
materialistic side which can never be completely
explained in scientific, intellectual, logical or
psychological terms. The teaching of *The Three
Signs of Being* is a case in point. Here is a strong
analytical approach which results in a self-evident
realization that can never be proved scientifically,
simply because it is a personal experience.

All that exists, according to the Buddha,
essentially has three characteristics:

- Impermanence (*anicca*)
- Unsatisfactoriness and suffering (*dukkha*)
- Not-self (*anatta*)

These characteristics are recognized when contemplating the body and mind. The most obvious manifestation of this is with thoughts. Contemplating the nature of thoughts will lead to the recognition that they are impermanent - they have a beginning and an ending; the same thought does not stay forever.

As thoughts continuously come and go, they are unreliable and unsatisfactory; they tell us one thing one day and another thing the next. There can be no lasting satisfaction in anything which is subject to change. One moment thoughts are pleasant and we feel pleasant, the next they are unpleasant and we feel bad.

The fact that thoughts come and go, also means that they are independent of us - we cannot control them and we do not own them. In which case, they are not really what 'I' am. We do not think of the coming and going of pain in the limbs as being what we really are, and there is no need to think of thoughts, which also come and go, as being what we are, either. The experience of thoughts is a constant, but the thoughts themselves are not. In this sense, therefore, it can be seen that thoughts are not our true selves, that which is permanent.

From the Buddhist perspective it would be
foolish to claim thought as being 'me', 'mine' or
'myself'. The same with the body – it is
impermanent and not what 'I' really am. Attachment
to the body with the idea of it being 'me' only leads
to a sense of unsatisfactoriness and suffering.

To put it yet another way, to be 'an individual' in
the way that we normally think of ourselves is to be
'unhappy'. When the three signs of being have
been fully penetrated and understood, then the
attachment to all thoughts of a 'self' cease, and so
does the suffering.

Four Noble Truths

It could be said that the Four Noble Truths is
Buddhism in a nutshell; it is the very basis of the
teaching, and some believe the study of Buddhism
is unnecessary beyond these four truths.

The truth of suffering

One faces the reality of one's own suffering. It is
not physical pain that is being referred to here; it is
mental suffering – anger, irritation, anguishing,
worrying, despairing, longing, wishing, hoping for a
person or an object or a condition which is not

present, or wishing to get rid of something that
is present.

The truth of the cause of suffering

One begins to see that suffering comes from
disliking what one has, desiring things to be
different, wishing to escape from something,
wishing to acquire or achieve something. Desire
itself is then seen to be the root cause of suffering,
rather than the object of desire.

The truth of the cessation of suffering

One realizes that resisting the pull to desire things
all the while, in large or small ways, is freedom
from suffering. To experience this as a reality is
nibbana – the cooling of the heat of wanting,
wishing, anguishing about things.

The truth of the way

It then becomes obvious that accepting or valuing
the moment for what it is, is freedom from desire,
and freedom from desire is freedom from suffering
within oneself. Freedom from suffering within
oneself is happiness, but it is a spiritual happiness,
not a conventional happiness. From a conventional
point of view, there can be no lasting happiness

⊙ Thai Buddha in earth-touching pose
© Photo: Richard St Ruth

because even if one has no pain or suffering within one's own life, the pain and suffering of others cannot be ignored and will destroy one's own peace of mind. Only when one sees that all beings are interdependent (see *The Twelve Links of Interdependence*) and that pleasure and pain always go hand in hand (there cannot be one without the other), will true happiness be found.

The way one lives is then consciously altered to match this understanding. Pleasure is not sought, though it comes naturally within one's life, nor pain shunned, though that also comes naturally within one's life. Instead, one comes to realize the perfection of life at any time beyond, behind, above, transcending pleasure and pain. This is a way of embracing the present moment, not rejecting it, a harmlessness and moral way of life that is generally presented as the noble eightfold path.

The Eightfold Path

The eight aspects of this path are:

- Right or perfect view
- Right intention
- Right speech
- Right action
- Right livelihood
- Right effort
- Right mindfulness
- Right concentration

This is not a linear path – first perfecting one's view about things before moving on to perfecting one's intentions and speech and so on. This is a way of living one's whole life. It is like saying: Try to live your life in the right way in everything you do.

The word 'right' or 'perfect', of course, is a subjective term, and that is what it is meant to be. There is no definition laid down of what is right; it is not a set of rules. What may be regarded as right effort for one person, for example, may be quite different for another. It is a question of deciding for oneself whether enough effort is being put into what one does, or whether there is a sense of laziness, or of making too much of an effort. There is a delicate balance to be found between too much and too little, and this is something to be discovered for oneself. The eightfold path is a life; it is one's whole way of life.

The Four Stages Towards Enlightenment

There are many attempts in Theravada Buddhism to name and categorize the levels of development possible for the practitioner. There is, for example, the teaching of the four stages.

The first stage of development is said to be the stream-enterer, the *sotapanna*. This is one who is free from the illusion of self, scepticism, attachment to rule and ritual, has unshakeable faith in the Buddha and his teaching, and firmly lives by the five moral precepts. It is believed that such a person will not be reborn more than seven more times before realizing deathlessness (*nibbana*), and will not be born into a state lower than the human realm.

A once-returner, a *sakadagamin*, is the second level of development. This is one who not only has the qualities of the stream-enterer, but has also overcome sensual desire and ill will in their gross forms. Such a person will not, it is said, be reborn more than one further time into the sensuous sphere.

A non-returner, an *anagamin*, is the third stage, and here one is wholly freed from the illusion of self, scepticism, attachment to rule and ritual, sensual desire, and ill will.

The final stage is to become a perfected holy one, an *Arahant*, and this is the highest ideal of a Theravada Buddhist. The *Arahant* is totally free from the belief in an individual self, scepticism, attachment to rules and rituals, sensual desire, resentment, craving for material and immaterial existence, arrogance, restlessness, and ignorance.

These stages are thought, by the more scholarly Buddhists, to be so pure and high that for the ordinary human being they are almost impossible to achieve, only the very finest adherents, perhaps, making it to even the first level. The more practice-oriented Theravadans, however, the meditators, usually view these stages as the consequence of practice in the moment rather than as personal fixed levels of attainment.

The Twelve Links of Dependent Origination (*paticcasamuppada*)

This, like all the teachings, is related to cause and effect, the workings of the joy and sorrow in our lives, the mechanics behind our lives, and the way to liberation from sorrow. What we experience can be divided into twelve states:

- Ignorance (*avijja*) or not knowing
- Volitional impulses (*samkhara*) or the impulse to take certain actions
- Consciousness (*vinnana*)
- Mind and body (*nama-rupa*)
- Six sense bases (*salayatana*) — eye, ear, nose, tongue, body, and mind
- Sense-impression (*phassa*)
- Feeling (*vedana*)
- Craving (*tanha*)
- Clinging (*upadana*)
- Becoming (*bhava*)
- Birth (*jati*)
- Ageing and death (*jaramarana*)

These twelve are linked together. There is no first or last link; this is a circular chain like a bracelet and each link conditions the links either side of it, one way or the other.

When there is ignorance about life and past conditioning, certain impulses will result; those impulses will cause particular kinds of consciousness to come into being; that consciousness will condition the way in which the mind and body function; the mind and body will condition the six senses, the way the eyes, ears, nose, tongue, body, and mind work; the six senses will condition the impressions or sensations that arise from seeing, hearing and so on; those impressions will condition the feelings which follow of like or dislike; these feelings will lead to craving for what is liked or craving to be rid of what is disliked; that craving will result in clinging to a particular desire; clinging will lead to existing in a certain way – a process of becoming this or that; this process of becoming will result in birth into conditions; and birth will inevitably lead to the deterioration or ageing of those conditions, and death. But death is a condition of ignorance, and so the process continues, round and round. There is no cutting off of the process here at death, whether death is seen in terms of something which takes place in a single moment, an hour, a day, or a lifetime.

The chain of dependent origination can be broken at any point. It is not an inevitable process that goes on and on. Through contemplation, through meditation, by treading the noble path, with the right intention and determination, that process of automatically going from one condition to the next can be stopped at any point. Life is not stopped by ending this process, of course; only birth into conditions of suffering cease; that is what the teaching is for – liberation.

Chapter 6

The Middle Way

Extremes

The Buddha lived the first part of his life in extreme comfort and luxury. His every whim was catered for, and yet he found that way of life cloying and nauseating; he felt like a prisoner. As a reaction to that, when he left home in search of truth, he swung to the other extreme and became an ascetic of the first order. He denied the body of what was unnecessary for survival, but also of what was needed by way of sleep and food, and he suffered the most wretched existence.

When, finally, at the point of death, he recognized the futility of what he was doing, he realized that both extremes were detrimental, and that a middle course had to be found, otherwise he would never reach the goal. It was from these experiences of the two extremes of pleasure and pain that the Buddha taught 'the middle way'.

⊙ *Statue of emaciated Buddha*

Transcending Dualities

In the materialistic sense, the middle way can be thought of as a balancing act between deprivation and overindulgence. The excesses that one might run to in one's everyday life are never specifically defined in the Buddhist teachings. This is a subjective path – each person finds his or her own way along it. Broadly speaking, it is a matter of not taking too much, of not being greedy or overindulging the senses, and of not denying too much, either. The clue as to whether one is treading the path correctly or not is whether the results of one's actions are wholesome or unwholesome.

In a spiritual sense, the middle way is resisting the temptation to grasp after truth, enlightenment, or liberation, and yet still going in that way. It is the transcending of all the dualities of pleasure and pain, love and hate, right and wrong, good and bad, me and you; the middle way is the way of nonduality.

No Buddhist Stand on Issues

There is no stand to take in Buddhism on specific issues. The onus is on the individual. Ideally, one follows one's own conscience and does whatever seems appropriate at the time.

The debate on abortion is a classic example. People may try to decide which camp to join – the anti-abortionists or the pro-abortionists. A Buddhist may join either of these camps and campaign one way or the other, or may not take a stand at all. From the point of view of Buddhism, this is treading the course of a living truth which acts according to conditions and a person's own sensitivities towards them. Answers to issues like abortion are not to be found in the Buddhist scriptures.

Chapter 7

Suffering & Release from Suffering

Samsara

In Buddhism it is said that, until one is awakened
to the truth of existence, the world that is
experienced is one of unsatisfactoriness, irritation,
suffering, sorrow or despair. Not only in obvious

⊙ *Buddha's footprint*

times of pain, loss and tragedy, is it like this, but even in moments of pleasure, achievement and success. Even at times when everything seems to be going well, an element of displeasure is to be found, an element of disappointment, a hidden fear that things may go wrong, a fear of losing a loved one, a fear of death. This strong or subtle sense of dissatisfaction with life is called *samsara*; it is where pleasures are fleeting and desire for them ever present.

Nibbana (Skt. Nirvana)

Then Buddhism talks about *nibbana*, and *nibbana* is the reverse of *samsara*. It is not a place or a particular condition that one arrives at, it is simply freedom from unsatisfactoriness; it is the other side of unsatisfactoriness and sorrow, and as such is happiness.

This kind of happiness is the result of no-dissatisfaction; it has nothing to do with pleasure or getting what one wants; it is simply lack of suffering.

Nibbana is the goal. It literally means 'cooling'. When we come out of the heat of anger, passionate longing, the hot drive for power, we become cool. The Buddha described *nibbana* as unborn, unconditioned, unmade. Its characteristics are awareness, peace, calm, selflessness, deathlessness, wisdom and compassion.

The Sun is Always Out

Happiness is a natural condition that prevails when suffering in all its forms is cleared away, a bit like the sun which comes out when the clouds are gone. The sun does not really come out at those times; the sun is always there; it is just that the clouds obscure it. This is like *samsara* in relation to *nibbana*. Happiness is always there, but sorrow obscures it. We do not have to find happiness; we just have to see past the unhappiness.

Two Sides of the Same Coin

Samsara and *nibbana* are two sides of the same coin; they should not be thought of as different places. They are both the same world, the same life, but lived from different perspectives.

Two people can experience similar things in life, and yet one can be in *nibbana* (feeling free, joyful, and at ease) and the other can be in *samsara* (feeling worried, upset and distressed). It is all to do with how life is lived, rather than what life presents to us.

Chapter 8

Kamma & Rebirth

Kamma (Skt. Karma)

In Buddhism freedom from suffering is regarded as the natural state, and so is wisdom and compassion. These are not learned or acquired attributes from the outside; they are the essential nature of all beings and all conditions. How is this known? It is known through the law of kamma, the nature of cause and effect. It is the Buddhist process of retribution.

Why do we feel unhappy? It may be because we have said or done something which has made us feel like that. We have said something to someone which we now regret. We find that we feel bad about it. We may try to justify it to ourselves, but we cannot and there is a vague sense of shame, guilt. This feeling is the result of what we have done. It is the kammic reaction. If we had not intended any harm to another, we would not be

⊙ *The Buddha's* parinibbana

feeling like this now. *Kamma* is quite simple and
obvious in that sense.

That is instant *kamma*, instant retribution.
There may be delayed *kamma*. Perhaps we did
something years ago as a child, the results of which
are just beginning to manifest. Perhaps we took a
spider and pulled all its legs off. Perhaps we told a

lie and got someone into trouble. At the time it did not feel too bad, but the mere thought of it now makes us cringe. That feeling, again, is *kamma* at work. The same is true in reverse – selfless actions bring good results. One may feel good about oneself, not in a narcissistic way, but there is a sense of feeling happy about what one has done.

These are simple examples, but the principle can be seen running right through everything we do. Some regard it as a power which is absolutely exact and precisely equal. I steal from you; someone else steals from me. I stab someone in the back, literally or metaphorically; someone does the same to me.

All beings are the owners of their deeds, the heirs of their deeds – their deeds are the womb from which they sprang, with their deeds they are bound up, their deeds are their refuge. Whatever deeds they do – good or evil – of such they will be the heirs.

The Buddha, from the *Anguttara-Nikaya*.

Not every difficulty in life is the result of bad causes, of course. We cannot make judgements when it comes to other people. Many things appear bad in the beginning, but turn out to be beneficial in the end. We develop and mature because of them. Wealth is not always good; poverty is not always bad. Illness is not always bad. We all get ill; it is what we do with it that matters.

Once we become aware of the principle, see it at work within our lives, then we realize that *kamma* is actively righting wrongs. These are not wrongs decreed by human beings in a court of law; these are wrongs decreed by nature. The laws of nature seem to be frighteningly just. Of course, there are many injustices in the world which are hard to explain in this way. But the law of *kamma* is not simplistic; it is very complex, and definitely not to be used as a judgement of others because we do not see the full picture.

We can only know *kamma* for ourselves; it is to be recognized as an active and powerful force within oneself, and then it can be trusted and used as a means of guidance in one's life.

In the same way that *kamma* may take months or years to come to fruition, so too, in the eyes of many Buddhists, the results of our actions may come in future lifetimes, or we may be now experiencing the results of something we did in past lifetimes. On a very materialistic level, the tendency is to believe that generosity, for example, in this life will bring riches in the next. But the Buddha was concerned with the spiritual path, not a materialistic one, and his teaching was related to wisdom and compassion, sorrow and liberation from sorrow, not on gaining success or riches in future lives.

⊙ *Reclining Buddha at Wat Chayamangkalaram, Penang*

Rebirth

Easterners are invariably convinced that this life is
not a one-off experience, that we have all lived
many lives in the past and will go on to live again
and again in the future, either in this earthly realm

or in others. In fact, many Easterners take this quite for granted and would find it extremely difficult to believe otherwise.

The average Westerner, on the other hand, has great difficulty in believing in more than one life, even though he or she would like to. After all, 'Where's the proof?' And so Westerners often believe in annihilation, feeling this to be more logical.

Both of these positions, however, are based on conditioning and the belief in a self – a self which either goes on forever, or a self which lives one little life and then comes to an end. Both of these, in Buddhism, are regarded as wrong views.

It is only after scrutinizing our lives inside and out that we come to realize that many of our beliefs are delusions; they are the products of conditioning as children and subsequently. The idea of oneself as an individual unit living inside a body is one of the crucial ones. Once this belief is recognized as being without foundation, then a wider perspective will begin to open up. This is when rebirth has meaning in the Buddhist sense.

Rebirth is life in flux beyond space and time. All thoughts are transcended, which means all ideas of being a particular person, living in a particular place, at a particular time, are dropped. The mundane mind sees this body and mind as a personal belonging and, in consequence, fears death. The Buddha went beyond that limited perspective and called himself the *Tathagata*, the 'thus come', the 'spontaneously arisen one', the 'one who is without birth and death', the 'one who was never born and will never die'. This is totally different from both the eternalist or nihilist views.

Birth itself is the delusion, that one lives inside this body and mind. Whenever one thinks that, or identifies with the body and mind in a personal way, then one is born into the world of suffering. This happens over and over again, and is what is meant by rebirth.

Birthlessness and Deathlessness

When one realizes that eternity is a view and annihilation is a view, both without foundation, then these notions and beliefs are dropped and another perspective comes into being, that of birthlessness and deathlessness. Life is experienced as a constant rebecoming process.

The Buddha taught of the futility of holding to views and, in particular, the view of eternity and annihilation. He held neither of these views himself and said that the truth lies within oneself – there is the all-knowing, all-seeing, wise and compassionate one. This transcendent wisdom and compassion is never born and never dies. This is what the Buddha's teaching is pointing to.

Buddhism acknowledges the birth and death of bodies and minds, but speaks of what is not born and does not die, which is the essence of what we really are, of what we are to ourselves in a deeply personal sense.

Unhelpful Questions

On various occasions the Buddha was asked whether the world was eternal or not, or whether there was life after death or not. At one time a wanderer by the name of Vacchagotta inquired, 'Are you of the view that the world is eternal?'

'No,' said the Buddha, 'I am not of that view.'

'Are you of the view that the world is not eternal?' continued Vacchagotta.

'No, I am not.'

'Are you of the view that the world is finite?'

'Not so.'

'That the world is infinite?'

'No.'

'Are you of the view that the life-principle and the body are the same?'

'No, I am not of that view.'

'That the life-principle is one thing and the body another?'

'No.'

'That the Tathagata* exists after dying?'

'No.'

'That the Tathagata does not exist after dying?'

'No.'

'That the Tathagata both exists and does not exist after dying?'

'No.'

'That the Tathagata neither exists nor does not exist after dying?'

' No, I am not of that view.'

Views and Opinions

The Buddha then made it clear that thinking that the world is eternal or not, or that he will continue after death or not, is holding a view, and views are nothing but fetters which are accompanied by anguish and distress. Views and opinions about

---

* *Tathgata*: A name the Buddha used to refer to himself; it literally means 'thus come'.

anything at all, said the Buddha, are not conducive to awakening, to *nibbana*. The questions were therefore unfit, unwise; they did not fit the case; they were being asked from the wrong perspective. It is not that he could not, or was simply refusing to answer them. The questions were simply the wrong questions and any answers to them would be misunderstood and misinterpreted.

The truth of existence, of life and death, is something to be experienced, not something to be thought about and set in concrete. And so the Buddha continued by saying, 'I do not have speculative views. What I do see is that such is material shape, such is the arising of material shape, such the going down of material shape; such is feeling, such is perception, such are the habitual tendencies, such is consciousness, such is the arising of consciousness, the going down of consciousness, and so forth. And I say that by the destruction, stopping, giving up, relinquishing all imaginings, all suppositions, the fundamental pride that "I am the doer," a Tathagata is freed, without clinging.'

'But, good Gotama,' continues Vacchagotta, 'where does a monk arise whose mind is freed like that?'

'"Arise," Vaccha, does not apply.'

'Well then, does he not arise?'

'The term "does not arise" does not apply.'

'Well then, does he both arise and not arise?'

'That does not apply either.'

'Well, does he neither arise nor not?'

'It doesn't apply.'

'Good Gotama, I am bewildered.'

'It is not surprising you are bewildered, Vaccha. This teaching (*dhamma*) is deep, difficult to understand and unattainable by mere reasoning. What do you think? If a fire were burning in front of you, would you know that it is burning?'

'Yes, I would.'

'But if someone were to ask you the reason for that fire burning, what would you say?'

'I would say that it was because of a supply of grass and sticks.'

'And if that fire were to be extinguished, would you know it had been extinguished?'

'Yes, I would know.'

'But if someone were then to ask you to which direction it had gone from here – to the east or west, north or south? What would you say?'

'I would say it does not apply. The fire burned because it was fuelled by grass and sticks. Once the fuel was used up, the fire went out.'

'Likewise, Vaccha, that material shape by which

one might recognize the Tathagata has been got rid of by the Tathagata, cut off at the root; it is no longer subject to arising again in the future. The Tathagata is freed from being denoted by material shape, Vaccha; he is immeasurable and as unfathomable as is the great ocean. "Arises" does not apply, nor does "does not arise", and so on. That feeling, that perception, those habitual tendencies, that consciousness by which one recognizes the Tathagata has been got rid of by the Tathagata, cut off at the root; it can come to no further existence and is not liable to arise again in the future.'

From sutta 72: *Discourse to Vacchagotta on Fire, Middle Length Sayings*

Past and Future Lives

Birth and death of a self is taught to be a delusion, but birth and death of form, feeling, perception, mental activities, and consciousness, are to be recognized as an ongoing process. The Buddha freely talks about past and future lives in this sense.

'Unimaginable, monks, is a beginning to the round of births. It is not easy to find a being who has not formerly been one's mother, father, brother, sister, son, daughter, during this long, long time.'

The Buddha, from the *Samyutta-Nikaya*

'Which do you think is more – the flood of tears, which, weeping and wailing, you have shed upon this long way, hurrying and hastening through this round of rebirths, united with the undesired, separated from the desired – this, or the waters of the four oceans?

'Long have you suffered the death of father and mother, of sons and daughters. And while you were suffering, you indeed shed more tears upon this long way than there is water in the four oceans.

'Long have you undergone suffering, undergone torment, undergone misfortune, and filled the graveyards full – truly, long enough to be dissatisfied with all the forms of existence, long enough to turn away and free yourselves from them all.'

The Buddha, from the *Samyutta-Nikaya*

The Buddha Talks of Recalling His Own Previous Existences

'Thus, with the mind composed, quite purified, I directed my mind to the knowledge and recollection of former habitations. I remembered one birth, two, three, four, a hundred thousand births, and many an aeon of integration and many an aeon of disintegration and many an aeon of integration-disintegration; such a one was I by name, having such and such a clan, such and such a colour, so was I nourished, such and such pleasant and painful experiences were mine, so did the span of life end. Passing from this, I came to be in another state where such a one was I by name. Passing from this, I arose here. Thus I remember various former habitations in all their modes and detail.'

The Buddha, from the *Majjhima-Nikaya*

He also said he could see the course of other beings:

'I comprehend that beings are mean, excellent, comely, ugly, well-going, ill-going, according to the consequences of their deeds, and I think, "Indeed these worthy beings who were possessed of wrong conduct in body, speech, thought, incurring deeds consequent on a wrong view – these, at the breaking up of the body after dying, have arisen in a sorrowful state. But these worthy beings who were possessed of good conduct in body, speech, thought, incurring deeds consequent on a right view – these, at the breaking up of the body after dying, have arisen in a good state."'

The Buddha, from the *Majjhima-Nikaya*

Eternity or Annihilation

At another time a monk by the name of Malunkyaputta was meditating and he thought, 'The Buddha has never told me whether the world is eternal or not. If he doesn't know the answer, he should say so. He hasn't told me whether the world is finite or infinite, or whether the soul is the same as the body, or whether the soul is one thing and the body another. He hasn't told me whether a Tathagata exists after death or not, or whether a Tathagata both exists and does not exist after death, or whether a Tathagata neither exists nor does not exist after death. If he knows these things, let him say so. And if he doesn't tell me, then I'll abandon the training and return to lay life.'

So Malunkyaputta went to the Buddha and asked him these questions. The Buddha said, 'Did I ever say, "Come and live the holy life under me and I will declare these things to you?"'

'No, venerable sir.'

'If anyone should decide not to lead the holy life under me until I say whether the world is eternal or not and so forth, it would still remain unsaid and, in the meantime, that person would die.'

From sutta 53: *Discourse to Malunkyaputta, The Middle Length Sayings*

The result of practising the Buddha's teachings
cannot be known at the beginning. Initially, therefore,
there may be a lot of hesitation about whether to do
what he suggests or even to embark on the practices:
'Should I be mindful during the day?' 'Should I be
aware of the way my mind works, the things I say
and do, the consequences of my actions?' 'Will it
work?' 'Is there any point to it?' 'Will I find liberation
from sorrow by adhering to the five precepts?'

The questions may be endless and they will be
endless unless one takes the trouble to find out for
oneself. One has to make that journey alone. The
Buddha gave a simile for this kind of doubt and
hesitation – the simile of the Poisoned Arrow.

The Poisoned Arrow

'Suppose, Malunkyaputta, a man were wounded by
an arrow thickly smeared with poison, and his friends
brought a surgeon to treat him. The man would say,
"I will not let the surgeon pull out the arrow until I
know whether the man who wounded me was a
noble or a brahmin or a merchant or a worker. I will
not let the surgeon pull out this arrow until I know
the name and clan of the man who wounded me,
until I know whether the man who shot me was tall
or short or of medium height, until I know whether

he was dark or golden-skinned, until I know whether the man lives in a village or a town or a city, until I know whether the bow that wounded me was a long bow or a crossbow, until I know whether the bowstring was made of fibre or reed or sinew or hemp or bark, until I know whether the shaft was wild or cultivated, until I know what kind of feathers the shaft was fitted wit, whether of vulture feathers, or a crow's or a hawk's or a peacock's or a stork's, until I know what kind of sinew the shaft was bound with, that of an ox or a buffalo or a lion or a monkey, until I know what kind of arrow it was that wounded me, whether it was hoof-tipped or curved or barbed or calf-toothed or oleander."

'None of this would be known to the man and in the meantime he would die. Malunkyaputta, if there is the view that the world is eternal, the holy life cannot be lived. The same with all the other views about the soul being the same as the body and the soul being one thing and the body another, and so forth. The holy life cannot be lived while holding these views. And whatever views one holds, there is birth, there is ageing, there is death, sorrow, pain, grief and despair, the destruction of which I prescribe here and now.'

These are truths to be realized, not to be believed in. They may seem to be paradoxical and difficult to understand, but it is only the words that are paradoxical, not the truths themselves.

Chapter 9

Buddhist Love

There are many forms of spiritual love. In Theravada Buddhism, four are referred to. They are called the Sublime Abodes (*Brahma-viharas*).

These are conditions of the mind which are greatly encouraged in the Theravada tradition. They are loving kindness (*metta*), compassion (*karuna*), altruistic or sympathetic joy (*mudita*), and equanimity (*upekkha*).

Loving Kindness

Loving kindness is the first state to be observed within oneself. There is no sensual passion involved in this kind of love. The word 'loving' is really just an emphasis on the kindness – a loving kindness, a deep kindness, a kindness which takes up all of one's heart and mind. It may also be referred to as boundless kindness.

⊙ *Wat Phrathat Doi Suthep, northern Thailand*

One begins by simply generating a feeling of loving kindness, and then directing it towards oneself. This might sound narcissistic, especially to the Western mind, but if one cannot feel kindness for oneself, there is absolutely no hope of feeling it for anyone else. This is an objective approach to who one is. One looks at oneself as 'a being' out there, someone to send loving kindness to.

This is a way of forgiving oneself for the wrongs one has done, or thinks one has done. Often we are full of guilt for its own sake; we have not done anything wrong at all. This kind of love clears away that kind of self-hatred. But, whether we have done anything wrong or not, we just feel a real kindness for ourselves.

That kindness is a sensation. It can be felt in the body, in the heart and mind. It may almost feel like an energy. After permeating oneself with this energy, this kindness, then one sends it out to the world in all directions. Or one thinks of a dear friend and sends the kindness to that person. Then one sends it to a neutral person, someone who brings up no feelings at all. And, finally, one sends loving kindness to a person one does not much like.

This is a particular practice in Buddhism, a particular meditation, and a very effective one.

Compassion

The next form of love in the Sublime Abodes is
compassion. This is a more refined love. It has no
personal element in it; it is lighter than kindness
yet more sublime. The compassion that one feels
towards oneself is less personal, perhaps, more
forgiving; it takes a broader perspective and is a
very sophisticated form of love.

As with the loving kindness, one then sends this
compassion out in all directions, or first to a friend,
then to a neutral person, then to someone who
wishes you harm or whom you dislike. Can you
keep that impersonal sense of compassion to all
those categories of beings? That is the object of
the exercise.

Sympathetic Joy

Sympathetic or altruistic joy is the third kind of
love. This is a feeling of happiness for joyful
experiences. Sometimes we do not feel comfortable
about feeling joyful ourselves; we do not think we
deserve it, or it makes us feel guilty. And so feeling
happy at our own joy can allow us to be
comfortable with it.

Most of all, however, we may have difficulty in feeling happy about other people's successes. There may be some jealousy mixed in with our feelings about the good fortune of others. Try feeling sympathetic joy for all beings in all directions, or to a friend first, then to a neutral person, and then to somone you do not like.

Can we be happy at the happiness of others? Do we feel jealous? These exercises make us realize how open- or mean-hearted we are.

Equanimity

The fourth sublime state, equanimity, is the most refined of all. This might almost sound like a state of nothing, a blank space, but in fact it is a selfless and powerful condition. This is completely impersonal. The idea of 'self' and 'other' do not enter into the picture here. This is beyond feelings and thoughts – a total stillness, complete peace. When this equanimity is directed towards oneself, there is stillness and peace, and when it is directed out to all beings, or to the different categories of beings, there is no difference of feeling to any of them.

Suffusing the World with Love

In the Pali suttas it is said:

With one's heart filled with loving kindness loving, one rests suffusing one quarter, the second, the third, the fourth. One rests suffusing the whole world, upwards, downwards, across, everywhere, always with a heart filled with loving kindness, abundant, without limits, without hate or ill will.

With one's heart filled with compassion, one rests suffusing one quarter, the second, the third, the fourth. One rests suffusing the whole world, upwards, downwards, across, everywhere, always with a heart filled with compassion, abundant, without limits, without hate or ill will.

. . . and so with sympathetic joy, and then with equanimity.

» Love for All Beings

A popular formula used for loving all beings indiscriminately:

Generate a sense of loving kindness and allow it to pervade your own body and mind. Have kindness for yourself. Wish happiness and freedom from suffering for yourself. Rest in that for a while.

Think of someone you love or like very much, a relative perhaps, or friend. Send loving kindness to them. Wish them all that is good and wish them freedom from suffering; suffuse them with feelings of good will.

Think of someone you hardly know or do not know at all, someone you have never spoken to, perhaps, or someone you feel entirely neutral about. Send them loving kindness. Wish them happiness and freedom from suffering.

Finally, think of someone you do not like, someone you are having difficulties with, a person who is being unkind to you, an enemy, perhaps. Feel the loving kindness within yourself and direct it towards that person. Try to bypass the normal feelings of hatred, irritation or enmity you have and send them loving kindness instead; wish them happiness and freedom from suffering.

Go through the procedure again with compassion, then sympathetic joy, and finally equanimity.

⊙ *The Buddha Preaching. One of the most famous Buddha statues, found at Sarnath, India, near to the site where he preached his first sermon*

Chapter 10

Monks, Nuns & Laypeople

Monks (*bhikkhus*)

Theravadan monks (*bhikkhus*) are a familiar sight in the cities, towns and villages of Sri Lanka, Thailand, and Myanmar, and can be easily identified by their saffron, bright yellow, or ochre-coloured robes and shaven heads.

Fully ordained monks are expected to keep 227 rules of the order. There are major rules, the obvious codes of practice, as in the Five Precepts (see page 43), and minor rules. Most of the 227 rules come into the minor category. There are thirty rules, for example, on how to receive and eat food – not smacking the lips when eating, for instance, and not making slurping noises.

More importantly, Theravada monks are celibate. They vow never to touch women, not even to shake their hands, and must not be alone in a room with a woman.

They are alms mendicants, i.e. they live on donations of food, medicines, and the few necessities that are required to maintain life. Their existence is, basically, one of renunciation and simplicity. If they are forest monks as distinct from city monks, they will spend a lot of time meditating and less time giving blessings and taking part in ceremonies. City monks, on the other hand, tend to do the reverse.

It is not uncommon to see monks distributing amulets – tiny Buddha images worn around the neck to ensure good fortune, provide protection, and bring wealth – or performing blessings of a distinctly un-Buddhist nature, such as blessing new businesses, ships, aeroplanes and cars. More understandably, they will be asked to bless a couple on their wedding day, chant prayers before cremations, and arbitrate in local or family disputes. But little of this will be found in the Buddhist scriptures; they are old traditions brought from pre-Buddhist times, or, modern equivalents.

Because monks are given food, the rule is that they must not eat after midday. This limits the burden on the lay population who provide it and, in theory, reduces the preoccupation they may have with eating. Also, monks are not allowed to purchase food, or purchase anything for that matter, nor may they ask for food or have a personal stock. Food remaining in the monk's bowl after his meal is to be disposed of; he is not permitted to save it till later.

He is, however, permitted to drink tea or coffee after the midday meal, as long as there is no milk in it, and small quantities of certain foods are allowed as 'medicine'. One or two pieces of cheese, for example, ginger, or dark chocolate can be taken, or drinks with soya milk. This is for the alleviation of hunger pains.

All necessities are to be offered at the temple or to monks on almsround. But, if you give anything, do not expect to be thanked. Monks are not permitted to do so, which does not mean to say they are not actually grateful. It is simply that personal relationships are not supposed to develop between monastics and laypeople, and one way of avoiding this is to restrict any intimate element involved in giving. Gifts are handed across with due ceremony for the benefit of the spiritual life of a 'monk', rather than for the benefit of a particular monk that one is becoming fond of. There is also the strong belief in the East that giving, especially to monks, is a virtue which brings its own reward so no thanks are necessary.

Theravada monks, also, do not work, apart from, perhaps, the daily chores of the monastery, do not grow their own food, do not act as messengers, do not earn their living in any way apart from being monks.

They are not supposed to touch money. When they travel, they usually need to be accompanied by either a layman or a male *anagarika* (page 101). The *anagarika* will carry the money to buy train tickets, make telephone calls or deal with anything which involves its handling.

A monk can travel alone, of course, if the ticket is given to him beforehand and if money is not needed for the journey. There is also some strange loophole, these days, which in some cases permits monks to carry credit cards, taking the position that pieces of plastic are not money.

Once ordained, a monk may leave the order at any time. He is not obliged to remain a monk for life. There is also an arrangement whereby one may take temporary ordination.

It is not uncommon for a man to become a Buddhist monk after retirement, or for men over twenty to take temporary ordination from five days to three months. Government offices, certain sections of the armed forces and some private companies may make temporary ordination possible by granting their employees three months' leave on full salary.

Nor is temporary ordination the exclusive privilege of any one class. Everyone from any walk of life may undertake to do it. Members of the royal family have been monks for short periods.

Nuns (*bhikkhunis*)

There are very few fully ordained Theravadan Buddhist nuns in the world, and most of these live outside Theravada countries. The order became extinct centuries ago,* and it is only very recently that the *bhikkhuni* (fully ordained nuns) order is being revived, and this not without a fight.

The attempt to restore the order of nuns has been unnecessarily blocked by the establishment monks, but now a handful of women with the backing of various sympathetic monks and scholars

* All but for a Chinese order which can be traced back, without interruption, to Sri Lankan nuns who emigrated to China in the fifth century CE.

have simply gone ahead with ordination ceremonies in America, Korea, and India, with plans for more. The struggle is on to end the long patriarchal reign. The Buddha was certainly for the emancipation of women and agreed to their ordination, but successive establishment monks have had difficulty in keeping up this attitude, preferring to revert to old cultural traditions. Now it looks as though a new age is dawning for Buddhist nuns, or a revival of the original one.

As yet, however, the majority of women who live as nuns are still not fully ordained. Some are ten-preceptors and wear saffron or dark brown, and this is the position of novice monks, but most are simply *anagarikas*, 'homeless ones'. They wear white and are, technically, laypeople.

The Eight Precepts of an *Anagarika*

To abstain from killing, stealing, engaging in sexual misconduct, unskilful speech, taking intoxicating drink or drugs, eating in the afternoons, wearing adornments and seeking entertainments, and sleeping in soft, luxurious beds.

There are male *anagarikas* too, but for the men this is usually a temporary position to enable them to serve the monks for a couple of years without the restrictions of the monastic order, and to give them time to decide whether to take the plunge and commit themselves to the life of a monastic.

In the East, female *anagarikas* live in nunneries and their lives are much the same as monks, except that they receive less support from laypeople and, therefore, tend to be more frugal and more humble. These women are often regarded as inferior beings – they are to sink to their knees, lower their heads, and put their two hands together in supplication when they encounter monks along the road. It is thought to be a blessing for a member of the family to be a monk – it is auspicious and good, karmically, for the family. Indeed, it is quite common for a man to become a monk for just three months, for the prestige of it, for the karmic merit that is hoped will result, and for the genuine spiritual and human values it is expected to bring to his life.

To have a nun (*anagarika*) in the family, however, may almost be a matter of shame. Many Easterners still believe that women are simply meant to have families, and that if they do not, it is because they cannot get husbands. The possibility that a woman may also wish to come away from the material world and lead a spiritual life simply does not come into it. These are cultural issues, of course, not to be mistaken for genuine Buddhist values. The women themselves do not necessarily care about status; they simply live modestly within the limits set for them.

In the West, however, where Buddhism is being taken up as a new way of life, these outmoded cultural prejudices are not being taken seriously. The women at Amaravati Buddhist Monastery in Britain, for example, though still technically not fully ordained, wear brown, are called nuns or sisters, and are on an equal footing with the monks.

Laypeople

The relationship between monks and laypeople in Theravada Buddhism is very strong. This type of Buddhism could not, in fact, exist with its present procedures without this link. Here is a way of mutual support – laypeople supply food, medicine, cloth for robes, and monks give spiritual support, blessings, and teachings to laypeople. Monks are not allowed to request anything and rely solely on the goodwill of the people.

The system works well and is so firmly established in most Theravadan countries that monks are usually amply provided for – depending on the wealth or poverty of the local people, that is.

Monasteries, also, often have facilities for laypeople to go into retreat for a short while. Usually the accommodation is basic and one has to abide by the Eight Precepts (see page 101). Whether a Westerner is permitted to stay in one of these establishments may depend upon the availability of someone to act as interpreter. It is not necessary to travel halfway round the world to go into retreat, however. These days there are ample opportunities in the West.

Theravada in the West

Theravada is not nearly as popular in the West as the other two major forms of Buddhism – Zen and Tibetan – but there is still a strong presence here in the form of temples and monasteries. Theravada depends much more on monastic situations and is, therefore, less 'portable' than the other forms of Buddhism. This is because of its strict disciplinary rules which make it almost impossible for monks and nuns to live in ordinary society. There is a great

dependency on laypeople and at the same time a
great divide.

Westerners, unfamiliar with the normal
courtesies and forms of respect, often innocently
cross the line of accepted behaviour. Women have
the most difficulty. Eastern women will honour the
monk's vow of celibacy by keeping their eyes
lowered in his presence and maintaining a
respectful distance. Western women, on the other
hand, may sit too close, wear short and skimpy
clothes, ask direct and inappropriate questions,
look straight into a monk's eyes, hand him things
directly instead of to a man first or to place them
onto a special cloth put out for the purpose,
inadvertently touch him on the arm or hand as one
does with friends, and so on. Most Westerners also
tend to sit in a relaxed or sloppy fashion compared
to the respectful Easterner, and even point their
fingers or the soles of their feet to Buddha-images
and monks, which is considered to be extremely
disrespectful.

Eastern monks in the West soon learn to live
with these harmless indiscretions, and Western
monks generally hardly notice, unless they are
being pursued by infatuated females or are
following the rules to the letter. Nevertheless,

ethnic Buddhists find it troubling to watch because monks are regarded as holy beings by virtue of the fact that they are wearing the robe. The robe is the symbol of the teaching, and the robe – not the man – is venerated and given the utmost respect.

Even if it is known that a particular monk flouts the rules, he is still generally respected by laypeople and called 'venerable'.

The 227 rules of discipline are intended to restrict a monk's activities, of course. Monastics are not supposed to be involved in personal relationships, or bear the trials and tribulations of family life. Their purpose is to seek liberation, abide by the precepts, perform ceremonies and, perhaps, to teach the *dhamma* (Buddhism).

Lay teachers have also emerged in the West. Many of these have been Theravadan monks or nuns in the past and disrobed for various reasons. Some have opened meditation centres which are run specially for laypeople. In many cases, the religious side of the tradition has been discarded, the concentration being on teaching a particular style of meditation known as *vipassana*, insight meditation.

These teachers and centres have become very popular and obviously answer a need for those who are interested in meditation but not in Buddhism. What is said to be at risk by more traditional Buddhists, however, is that by watering Buddhism down in this way, people are deprived of its deeper truth.

Going on Retreat

Buddhists who meditate will want to go into retreat at some time in their lives, and this is the ideal situation for deepening the practice.

When you step over the threshold for the first time, however, you might wonder why you have come! The measured pace of the monks, nuns, and other meditators, the silence, the lack of food after midday, the getting up at unearthly hours – suddenly all these things seem pointless and foolish. Do you stay, or do you flee? Do you immediately start counting the hours and days to departure time? A good many people find themselves doing that on their first retreat, or at least for the first couple of days; and then suddenly you may find yourself into it and reaping the benefits.

It takes time to orientate yourself into what for most people will be an alien way of life – up at the

crack of dawn, or before, sitting cross-legged on a
cushion on the floor, knees aching, back aching,
wondering why you are not at home, tucked up in a
nice warm bed. Then it is time for breakfast (one of
the high spots of the day?), then maybe an hour's
work (one of the low spots?) – chopping
vegetables in the kitchen, pulling weeds in the
garden, cleaning toilets, cleaning windows . . .
whatever.

Then back to the meditation room, back to the
cushion – another session of facing yourself,
looking at your own fears, anxieties, and feelings of
inadequacy, maybe feeling depressed, maybe
hating yourself for wanting to go home. You get
back to watching the breath in your mind's eye –
watching, being aware, feeling the rise and fall of
the abdomen, knowing the breath as it comes in
and goes out, feeling your whole being become
calm and at ease, solid, suddenly being totally at
peace with the world, suddenly not caring about
stray aches and pains in the body, suddenly not
worrying about all those things.

You hear the birds singing in the silence; you
have arrived in the present; you are at-one with the
moment – thoughts transcended, self transcended

— gone is the sense of being a separate individual living in a body in the world. The world is as it is; there is a sense of awakening to something you have always known but never centred upon or taken much notice of.

The monk rings the bell, the session is ended — what a beautiful sound.

Chapter 11

Holy Places, Holy Objects, Holy Days

India

The main Buddhist pilgrimage sites are in India – Bodh Gaya where the Buddha became enlightened under 'the tree'*, Sarnath where he gave his first teachings, Shravasti where he often taught, Kushinagar where he died (or more accurately passed into *parinibbana*†), and Lumbini, which is in present-day Nepal, where the Buddha was born.

There are many Buddhist temples, monuments and shrines around the world, but Northern India is the place for reflecting on the Buddha's life and teachings. There is, therefore, a constant stream of pilgrims passing along the route where the Buddha trod.

Countries which have had a long and established Buddhist presence are also popular places of pilgrimage, and also popular tourist attractions.

---

* The descendant still remains.
† *Parinibbana:* the complete going down of individuality and rebirth –
  not to be confused with annihilation or extinction.

⊙ *Paying respects to Buddha*

Sri Lanka

One of the most important religious treasures in Sri Lanka is housed in the Dalada Maligawa, the Temple of the Tooth, in Kandy. The tooth contained in this temple is believed to be a relic of the

⊙ *Golden stupa in the temple of the Emerald Buddha, Bangkok*

Buddha and therefore very sacred. Daily ceremonies of homage are performed to it, and every August, it is brought from the temple and carried round the city in a grand torch-lit procession (see page 122).

Kandy is the monastic centre of Buddhism in Sri Lanka. Numerous *stupas*, however, are to be found in various parts of the countryside

The *Stupa*

A most important and venerated Buddhist monument is the *thupa* (better known by its Sanskrit term: *stupa*). Originally these were mounds of earth containing the ashes or relics of the Buddha, of other holy beings, of objects used by the Buddha, or perhaps some sacred texts. Sometimes they were constructed simply to commemorate significant events in the life of the Buddha, as in the case of those at Lumbini, Bodh Gaya, Kushinagar, Sarnath and so on – places where the Buddha lived and taught. But *stupas* can be seen all over the Buddhist world, a few even in the West.

They have taken on different shapes in different countries. Sri Lankan and Thai *stupas* have kept to the original design of the basic Indian version, perhaps the most famous of which can be seen at Sanchi in central India. The Great Sanchi Stupa probably dates from Ashoka's* time.

As holy objects, *stupas* are circumambulated clockwise three times as a form of devotion and respect. Some people slowly walk around them contemplatively, some chant mantras or *suttas* as they go, some bow and light incense. It can be a very moving experience.

Apart from the many old and venerated *stupas* in Sri Lanka, there are numerous awe-inspiring and large Buddha sculptures – at Aukana and Buduruvagala, for example, and the Gal Vihare complex of seated, standing and reclining Buddhas sculpted in granite.

Buddha-Statues

Buddha-images are venerated objects before which Buddhists will bow. It is not a question of bowing down to a human being or a god, however, when Buddhists bow to a Buddha-image. The form represents the teaching. These statues are not worshipped. In fact, nothing is essentially

* A warrior King turned Buddhist of the third century BCE

worshipped in Buddhism apart from the truth.

In the very early days, the Buddha was often represented by an empty space, a footprint, a lotus, an eight-spoked wheel representing the eightfold path (see page 56), and so on. Iconic representations of the Buddha have been found from the same period, putting paid to the theory that Buddha-images did not appear until much later.

Some of the very earliest Buddha-images were influenced by the Greeks in northeast India. Indeed, it would be easy to mistake one of these representations for a Greek figure. Gradually, however, the artists began to give the statues Indian characteristics and the positions became standardized.

As Buddhism spread around the world, the features changed according to the nationality of the artist. It is relatively easy to identify the origin of a Buddha-image just by looking at the face. In the West, however, we do tend to like our Buddha-images with Eastern faces – Buddhas with Western faces somehow lose their mystique, though they do exist.

Buddhist art and art history is extensive and an entire study unto itself as can be seen from the contents of numerous museums and temples

⊙ Image of Sariputta, one of the chief disciples of the Buddha

around the world. As far as the average Buddhist is concerned, however, historical pilgrimage sites and objects on the shrine are to be used for spiritual purposes. They are for contemplating the life of the Buddha, his teachings, and their own lives.

People usually take great care in choosing a Buddha-image for themselves. The face, whatever its specific features or country of origin, is not meant to be just a human face or even a male face – many have distinctly feminine qualities – it is to express deep wisdom and compassion. This means that artists need to experience those qualities within themselves and have a sense of the mystery of existence while they are producing them. Otherwise the result will be poor. Consequently, there are relatively few really moving and inspiring images of the Buddha to be found, but when you see one, you will know whether it works for you.

It can be a very powerful experience reflecting upon such an object; it can be like reflecting upon your own mind and may result in bringing out the wisdom and compassion that is already within your own being.

Among other interesting pilgrimage sites in Sri Lanka is a cave temple – Dambulla, or Golden Rock, which dates back to the first century BCE and contains a large collection of Buddha statues – and, at Anuradhapura, the oldest historically documented tree in the world. This is believed to have been grown from a sapling of the tree under which the Buddha attained enlightenment in India. The sapling was sent to Sri Lanka as a gift from Emperor Ashoka shortly after the introduction of Buddhism to the country in about 250 BCE.

Thailand

Thailand has about twenty-seven thousand Buddhist temples, the majority of which are in the countryside. The Temple of the Emerald Buddha in the precincts of the Royal Palace in Bangkok, however, is one of the most sacred.

The Emerald Buddha is, in reality, carved from green jade*. According to legend, in 1434 CE lightning struck a pagoda in northern Thailand and a Buddha statue covered with stucco was found inside. The image was brought into the abbot's residence and one day he noticed that the stucco on the nose had flaked off and the image inside was green in colour. He removed all the stucco and

* The word 'emerald' means 'green' in Thai

found the Emerald Buddha. The lap of the Buddha is 48.3 cm wide and the height, including the base, is 66 cm.

This famous image has been stolen and recovered many times over the centuries, and was placed at its present site in 1784. Many wonderful treasures are also preserved in the temple museum.

Myanmar (Burma)

Myanmar is not the easiest country to visit, but it has countless Buddhist treasures within its borders. The golden Shwedagon Pagoda in Yangon (Rangoon) is regarded as the holiest site. Legend has it that the original stupa was built to enshrine eight of Buddha's hairs. Today's monument was built in the eighteenth century and is surrounded by statues, temples, shrines, images and pavilions. Its hundred-metre spire is sheathed in eight thousand gold plates and crowned with more than five thousand diamonds as well as other precious stones.

There are also numerous pagodas and temples in Mandalay, and Bagan (Pagan) has been described as one of the wonders of Asia with about five thousand temples on the banks of the Ayeyarwady (Irrawaddy) river.

Other impressive sites are at Bago (Pega) where a 55 metre (180 ft) long, reclining Buddha is to be found, and the Kyaiktiyo Pagoda, northeast of Yangon, is unusual in that it is delicately balanced on top of a massive gold-leafed boulder on the edge of a cliff.

Moon Days and Ceremonial Days (*uposatha*)

The phases of the moon are of special significance in the Theravada tradition.

For monastics, full moon and new moon days always mark the confession and recitation of the *Patimokkha* (rules of the order). Specific full moon days, however, are times of celebration for everyone.

On days like these, in many monasteries, physical labour (construction projects or repairs) is curtailed, laypeople bring food offerings, dress in their finest, listen to monks chanting and to teachings, practise meditation, circumambulate *stupas*, possibly with incense and candles, and generally renew their commitment to the practice.

The most important holiday is *Vesakha Puja*, celebrated on the full moon day of May. It is to commemorate three events simultaneously – the birth, enlightenment, and *parinibbana* (passing away) of the Buddha. Temples throughout the country are crowded with people. This is a joyful family occasion, filled with great excitement and renewed vows.

Other full moon holy days include:

Magha Puja – January/February
Commemoration of the spontaneous gathering of 1,250 disciples to hear the Buddha teach.

Asalha Puja – June/July

The celebration of the Buddha's first sermon to his first five disciples. This is immediately followed by the three-month rains retreat (*vassa*) which commences on the following day. (*Vassa* occurs during the Asian monsoon season and is a time for monks to stay in their monasteries, to study and to meditate.)

Kathina – October/November

A time when donations are made to the *sangha* of robe cloth and other requisites.

Esala Perahera – July/August

Sri Lanka holds another major event in the city of Kandy, called *Esala Perahera*, which falls in July/August. This is a most spectacular pageant with ten days of dancing and drumming, its climax being a great procession with decorated elephants, honouring the sacred tooth relic.

⊙ Eighteenth-century Bronze Buddha from Myanmar (Burma) wearing a crown and royal attire

Appendix 1

The Buddha's Words on Loving Kindness
(*Metta Sutta*)

The following is one of the most popular texts, especially with laypeople, and epitomizes Theravada's distinctly gentle characteristic.

Those who are ready for the goal,
As they draw near to that destination of calm –
They will be able, straight, yes, truly straight,
Gentle in speech and mild, without conceit.

They will be contented, easily satisfied,
Be of few needs and frugal in their ways;
Their senses will be calm and appropriate,
Not coveting, nor bold within people's homes.

They will never act in a mean way,
So that the perceptive would want to condemn them.
Their wish will be – 'May all beings be happy and safe,
And come at last to inner happiness!

'All beings who exist –
The weak and the strong, the tall and large,
The short and middle-sized – omitting none –
The little creatures and the very great –

'All beings who are seen, all those unseen,
Those that live far away, those that live nearby,
Those that are here and those that seek to be –
May all come to inner happiness!

'Let none mislead another,
Nor despise anyone in any place;
From quarrel or from enmity let none
Wish ill to any other being whatever.

'Even as a mother watches over her child,
Her only child, as long as she lives,
So, truly, for every being
Arouse a boundless heart.

'Arouse a heart of boundless kindness
For all things and all creatures –
Upwards and downwards and across the world.
Unhindered, free of hate and enmity.'

And as they stand or walk or sit or lie down,
Till overcome by drowsiness, let them
Devote themselves to this mindfulness –
'Sublime abiding', is this state called.

When beings are free from views,
Dwell in virtue, are endowed with insight,
Have finished with greed for pleasures,
Then they will never again go to birth.

From the *Sutta-Nipata*, vv. 143–152

The Greatest Blessing (*Mangala Sutta*)

On another occasion, when the Buddha was staying near Savatthi, a celestial being (*deva*) came to him and said, 'Many celestial beings and human beings have thought about blessings, longing for good things, but what is the greatest blessing?'

The Buddha said, 'To follow the wise, not to follow the foolish, to respect those worthy of respect – this is the greatest blessing.

To live in a fair place, to have performed good deeds in the past, to have set oneself on the right path – this is the greatest blessing.

To learn, become skilled and train in discipline, to use speech wisely – this is the greatest blessing.

To care for parents and family, to follow a peaceful livelihood – this is the greatest blessing.

To be generous and to tread the way of truth, to care for kin, and to perform blameless deeds – this is the greatest blessing.

To abstain from doing wrong, to be restrained in one's zeal for things – this is the greatest blessing.

To feel reverence, humility, contentment and gratitude, to hear truth in due season – this is the greatest blessing.

To have patience, to use kind words, to see good people, to converse on reality – this is the greatest blessing.

To have great energy in the holy life, to discern noble truths, to know the cooling of suffering – this is the greatest blessing.

To be unmoved when touched by the world, to be free of grief, to be free of faults, to be secure – this is the greatest blessing.

Those who live like this do not experience defeat; they are happy wherever they go – theirs is the greatest blessing.'

From the *Sutta-Nipata*, vv. 258-269

Appendix 2

Satipatthana Sutta

The following text is one of the most important of all the Buddha's teachings. It is regarded as the classic meditation sutta.

Thus have I heard. At one time the Buddha was staying among the Kuru people in a town called Kammassadhamma. While he was there, he addressed the monks: 'There is this one way, for the purification of beings, for the overcoming of sorrows and griefs, for the going down of sufferings and miseries, for winning the right path, for realizing *nibbana*, that is to say, the four applications of mindfulness. What are the four?

'A person lives contemplating the body in the body, ardent, clearly conscious of it, mindful of it so as to control covetousness and dejection in the world; a person contemplates the feelings* in the feelings, the mind in the mind, and the mental objects in the mental objects, ardent, clearly conscious of them, mindful of them so as to control covetousness and dejection in the world.

'And how does one live contemplating the body in the body? One who is forest-gone or gone to the root of a tree or to an empty place, sits down cross-legged, holding the back erect, arousing mindfulness in front of one. Mindful one breathes in, mindful one breathes out. Breathing in a long breath one

*The three feelings; of pleasure, pain and those that are neutral

comprehends, "I am breathing in a long breath"; breathing out a long breath one comprehends, "I am breathing out a long breath"; breathing in a short breath one comprehends, "I am breathing in a short breath"; breathing out a short breath one comprehends, "I am breathing out a short breath." One trains oneself, thinking, "I shall breathe in experiencing the whole body." One trains oneself, thinking, "I shall breathe out experiencing the whole body." One trains oneself, thinking, "I shall breathe in tranquillizing the activity of the body." One trains oneself, thinking, "I shall breathe out tranquillizing the activity of the body."

'It is like a clever turner who, making a long turn, comprehends, "I am making a long turn"; or when making a short turn comprehends, "I am making a short turn." Even so does one who is breathing in a long breath comprehend, "I am breathing in a long breath", etc.

'In this way, a person lives contemplating the body in the body internally, or contemplating the body in the body externally, or contemplating the body in the body internally and externally. Or a person contemplates origination-things in the body, or dissolution-things in the body, or origination-and-dissolution things in the body. Or, thinking, "There is the body," one's mindfulness is established precisely to the extent necessary just for knowledge, just for remembrance, and one lives independently of and not grasping anything in the world.

'And again, when walking, one comprehends, "I am walking"; when standing still, one comprehends, "I am standing still"; when sitting down, one comprehends, "I am sitting down"; or when lying down, one comprehends, "I am lying down." So that however one's body is disposed one comprehends that it is like that.

'And again, such a person, when setting out or returning is one acting in a clearly conscious way; when looking in front or looking around, has bent in or stretched out the arm, is carrying the outer cloak, bowl and robe, is eating, drinking, chewing, tasting, obeying the calls of nature, walking, standing, sitting, asleep, awake, talking, or silent, that person is one acting in a clearly conscious way.

'And again, such a person reflects on precisely this body itself, encased in skin and full of various impurities, from the soles of the feet up and from the crown of the head down, that, "There is connected with this body, hair of the head, hair of the body, nails, teeth, skin, flesh, sinews, bones, marrow, kidneys, heart, liver, membranes, spleen, lungs, intestines, mesentery, stomach, excrement, bile, phlegm, pus, blood, sweat, fat, tears, serum, saliva, mucus, urine."

'It is like a double-mouthed provision bag that is full of various kinds of grain such as kidney beans, peas, sesamum, rice; and a keen-eyed person, pouring them out, were to reflect: "That's kidney beans, that's peas, that's sesamum, that's rice." Even so does one reflect on precisely this body itself, encased in skin and full of various impurities, from the soles of the feet up and from the crown of the head down.

'And again, one reflects on this body according to how it is placed or disposed in respect of the elements, thinking, "In this body there is the element of extension, of cohesion, of heat, and of motion." Even as a skilled butcher, having slaughtered a cow, might sit displaying its carcass at a crossroads, so does one reflect on this body itself according to how it is placed or disposed in respect of the elements.

'And again, a person might see a body thrown aside in a cemetery, dead for one, two or three days, swollen, discoloured, decomposing; that person focuses on this body itself, * thinking, "This body, too, is of a similar nature, a similar constitution. It has not got past that state of things."

'And again, a person might see a body thrown aside in a cemetery, and being devoured by crows, ravens, vultures, wild dogs, jackals or various small creatures; that person focuses on this body itself, thinking, "This body, too, is of a similar nature, a similar constitution. It has not got past that state of things."

'And again, one might see a skeleton with some flesh and blood, sinew-bound, or fleshless but blood-bespattered, sinew-bound, or without flesh and blood, sinew-bound, or the bones scattered here and there, no longer held together – here a bone of the hand, there a foot bone, here a leg bone, there a rib, here a hip bone, there a backbone, here the skull.

And again, one might see a body thrown aside in a cemetery – the bones white like sea shells, a heap of dried up bones more than a year old, the bones gone rotten and reduced to powder.

* i.e. on his own body.

One focuses on this body itself, thinking, "This body, too, is of a similar nature, a similar constitution. It has not got past that state of things." Thus one lives contemplating the body in the body internally, externally, or internally and externally. Or one contemplates origination-things in the body, or dissolution-things in the body, or origination-dissolution-things in the body. Or, thinking, "There is the body," one's mindfulness is established precisely to the extent necessary just for knowledge, just for remembrance, and one fares along independently of and not grasping anything in the world.

'How does one live contemplating the feelings in the feelings? While one is experiencing a pleasant feeling one comprehends, "I am experiencing a pleasant feeling"; while experiencing a painful feeling one comprehends, "I am experiencing a painful feeling"; while experiencing a feeling that is neither painful nor pleasant one comprehends, "I am experiencing a feeling that is neither painful nor pleasant." While experiencing a pleasant feeling in regard to material things one comprehends, "I am experiencing a pleasant feeling in regard to material things"; while experiencing a pleasant feeling in regard to nonmaterial things one comprehends, "I am experiencing a pleasant feeling in regard to nonmaterial things." While experiencing a painful feeling in regard to material and nonmaterial things, and while experiencing a feeling that is neither painful nor pleasant in regard to material and nonmaterial things one comprehends it as it is. Thus one lives contemplating feelings in the feelings internally, externally, or internally and externally. Or one contemplates origination-things in the feelings, or dissolution-things in the feelings, or origination-dissolution-things in the feelings. Or, thinking, "There is feeling," one's mindfulness is established precisely to the extent necessary just for knowledge, just for remembrance, and one lives independently of and not grasping anything in the world.

'How does a person live contemplating mind in the mind? One knows intuitively the mind with attachment as a mind with attachment; one knows intuitively the mind without attachment as a mind without attachment, the mind with hatred as a mind with hatred, the mind without hatred as a mind without hatred, the mind with confusion as a mind with confusion, the mind without confusion as a mind without confusion; one knows intuitively the mind that is contracted* as a mind that is contracted, the mind that is distracted† as a mind that is distracted, the mind that has become great as a mind that has become great, a mind that has not become great as a mind that has not become great, the mind with some other mental state superior to it as a mind with some other mental state superior to it, the mind with no other mental state superior to it as a mind with no other mental state superior to it, the mind that is composed as a mind that is composed, the mind that is not composed as a mind that is not composed; and one knows intuitively the mind that is freed as a mind that is freed, or the mind that is not freed as a mind that is not freed.

* The mind fallen into sloth and torpor.
† Accompanied by restlessness.

Thus one lives contemplating the mind in the mind internally, externally, or internally and externally. Or one lives contemplating origination-things in the mind or dissolution-things in the mind, or origination-dissolution-things in the mind. Or thinking, "There is mind," one's mindfulness is established precisely to the extent necessary just for knowledge, just for remembrance, and one lives independently of and not grasping anything in the world.

'And how does a person live contemplating mental objects in mental objects? A person does this from the point of view of the five hindrances. When a subjective desire for sense pleasures is present, one comprehends that one has a subjective desire for sense pleasures; or when a subjective desire for sense pleasures is not present one comprehends that one has no subjective desire for sense pleasures. And in so far as there comes to be an uprising of desire for sense pleasures that had not arisen before, one comprehends that; and in so far as there comes to be a getting rid of desire for sense pleasures that has arisen, one comprehends that. And in so far as there comes to be no future uprising of desire for the sense pleasures that has been got rid of, one comprehends that. The same with ill will, sloth and torpor, restlessness and worry, and doubt. It is thus that one lives contemplating mental objects in mental objects internally, externally, or internally and externally. Or one lives contemplating origination-things in mental objects, or dissolution-things in mental objects, or origination-things and dissolution-things in mental objects. Or, thinking, "There are mental objects," one's mindfulness is established precisely to the extent necessary just for knowledge, just for remembrance, and one lives independently of and not grasping anything in the world. It is thus that a person contemplates mental objects in mental objects from the point of view of the five hindrances.

'And again, one lives contemplating mental objects in mental objects from the point of view of the five groups of grasping. One thinks, "Such is material shape, such is the arising of material shape, such is the setting of material shape; such is feeling, such the arising of feeling, such the setting of feeling; such is perception, such the arising of perception, such the setting of perception; such are the tendencies, such the arising of the tendencies, such the setting of the tendencies; such is consciousness, such the arising of consciousness, such the setting of consciousness."

'And again, a person lives contemplating mental objects in mental objects from the point of view of the six internal-external sense-bases. One comprehends the eye and material shapes, and the fetter that arises dependent on both. One comprehends the uprising of the fetter not arisen before, the getting rid of the fetter that has arisen, and the non-uprising in the future of the fetter that has been got rid of. The same with the ear and sounds, the nose and smells, the tongue and flavours, the body and tactile objects, and the mind and mental objects.

'And again, a person lives contemplating mental objects in mental objects from the point of view of the seven links in awakening. When the link in awakening that is mindfulness is present internally one comprehends that one has mindfulness; when the link in awakening that is mindfulness is not internally present one comprehends that one has no mindfulness. And in so far as there is an uprising of the link in awakening that is mindfulness that had not uprisen before, one comprehends that; and in so far as there is completion by the mental development of the uprisen link in awakening that is mindfulness, one comprehends that. The same with the link in awakening that is investigation of mental objects, and with the link in awakening that is energy, rapture, serenity, concentration and equanimity.

'And again, a person lives contemplating mental objects in mental objects from the point of view of the four noble truths. A person comprehends as it really is, "This is anguish; this is the arising of anguish; this is the stopping of anguish; this is the course leading to the stopping of anguish." It is thus that one lives contemplating mental objects in mental objects internally, externally, or internally and externally. Or one contemplates origination-things in mental objects, or dissolution-things in mental objects, or origination-things and dissolution-things in mental objects. Or, thinking, "There are mental objects," one's mindfulness is established precisely to the extent necessary just for knowledge, just for remembrance, and one lives independently of and not grasping anything in the world.

'Whoever should develop these four applications of mindfulness for seven years, one of two fruits is to be expected – either profound knowledge here-now or, if there is any residuum remaining, the state of nonreturning. Let be the seven years. Whoever should develop these four applications of mindfulness for six, five, four, three, two, or for one year, for seven months, or for six, five, four, three, two months, for one month, or for half a month, one of two fruits is to be expected – either profound knowledge here-now or, if there is any residuum remaining, the state of nonreturning. Let be the half month. Whoever should develop these four applications of mindfulness for seven days, one of two fruits is to be expected – either profound knowledge here-now or, if there is any residuum remaining, the state of nonreturning.

'What has been spoken in this way has been spoken in reference to this, "There is this one way for the purification of beings, for the overcoming of sorrows and griefs, for the going down of sufferings and miseries, for winning the right path, for realizing *nibbana*, that is to say, the four applications of mindfulness."

Thus spoke the Buddha. Delighted, the monks rejoiced in what the Lord had said.

From the *Satipatthanasutta, Majjhima-Nikaya*

Glossary

Ajahn: (Also spelt *achaan* and in other ways.) Teacher or senior monk.

Anagarika: A homeless one; one who wears white and is still, technically, a layperson, who lives in a monastery and keeps the eight precepts – refraining from killing, stealing, sexual misconduct, unskilful speech, taking intoxicating drink and drugs, food in the afternoon, adornments and entertainments, and sleeping in soft beds.

Arahant: A perfected holy one; one who is free from scepticism, attachment, sensual desire, resentment, craving for existence, arrogance, restlessness, and ignorance; the highest ideal of a Theravadan Buddhist.

Bhikkhu: Theravada Buddhist monk who lives a life of renunciation and simplicity as an alms mendicant according to the 227 rules of the order.

Buddha: Awakened; Siddhattha Gotama became awakened to the reality of life and was from then on known as the Buddha.

Dana: Giving; namely, giving food, medicine or robes to monks and nuns.

Deva: Celestial or heavenly being; a being who lives in a heavenly realm, is generally invisible, but who is still subject to birth, ageing, and death, the cycle of existence, and to conditions of unsatisfactoriness.

Dhamma: This word is used for many things – the teaching, all material objects, thoughts, feelings, the law of how the cosmos works from a meditator's point of view.

Dukkha: Souring, suffering in *samsara*, unsatisfactoriness, anguish, anxiety, fear, sorrow, grief. At first glance this seems a very negative thing and the Buddha's first noble truth that all life is *dukkha* is often taken as a negative statement, but from the Buddhist perspective it is simply the realization of the way things are under certain circumstances.

Hinayana: Small vehicle or way. A derogatory term used by some Mahayana Buddhists to describe Theravada.

Kamma: Actions by body, speech and mind, and the ripening of those actions into various states of being; good action leading to good result; bad action leading to bad result – in this life, in the next birth, or in later births.

Nibbana: The total extinction of all suffering.

Nun: In the East technically still an *anagarika* (not fully ordained and wearing the white of a layperson), but in reality living as do the monks (*bhikkhus*). There is a British order of nuns who have begun to cross the divide by wearing brown and taking on more precepts.

Parinibbana: The complete cessation of individuality and rebirth – not to be thought of as annihilation or extinction.

Samsara: The world of unsatisfactoriness and suffering; the world of greed, hatred and delusion; the round of rebirths into the realms of existence.

Sangha: Community or assembly; *Bhikkhu-sangha*: Community of monks.

Tathagata: Thus come; the one who neither comes nor goes. A term the Buddha used to describe himself.

Thupa (*Stupa*, Sanskrit; *dagoba*, Sinhalese; *choten*, Tibetan): Structures large or small which contain ashes or relics of holy persons or holy texts. In China and Japan they became the pagoda.

Vihara: A dwelling place; residence for monks; maybe a Buddhist retreat or monastery.

Further Reading

Dhammapada, Jack Austin, Buddhist Society, London, 1945.

Heartwood of the Bodhi Tree, Buddhadasa Bhikkhu, Wisdom, 1994.

The Middle Length Discourses of the Buddha, trans. Bhikkhu Nanamoli, Wisdom,!995.

The Mind and the Way: Buddhist Reflections of Life, Ajahn Sumedho, Rider, 1996.

Mindfulness in Plain English, Venerable Henepola Gunaratana, Wisdom, 1992.

Midfulness with Breathing, Buddhadasa Bhikkhu, Wisdom, 1997.

A Still Forest Pool: The Insight Meditation of Achaan Chah, Jack Kornfield and Paul Breiter, Quest Books, 1985.

Thus Have I heard: The Long Discourses of the Buddha, Trans. Maurice Walshe, Wisdom, 1987.

Bibliography

Buddhist Dictionary: Manual of Buddhist Terms and Doctrines, Nyanatiloka, The Corporate Body of the Buddha Educational Foundation, Taiwan, 1970.

The Buddhist Handbook, John Snelling, Rider, Revised edition 1998.

The Buddhist Monastic Code: The Patimokkha Training Rules, Mahamakuta Educational Council, Buddhist University, Thailand, 1993.

Flammarion Iconographic Guides: Buddhism, Louis Frederic, Flammarion, 1995.

Introduction to Buddhism, Diana St Ruth, Buddhist Publishing Group, 1988.

The Middle Length Sayings (Majjhima-Nikaya), Vols. I–III, Trans. I.B. Homer, Pali Text Society, 1967.

Rebirth, Buddhist Publishing Group, 1986

The Rider Encyclopaedia of Eastern Philosophy and Religion, Rider, 1989.

Satipatthana Sutta: The Buddha's Teaching of Mindfulness, trans. I.B.Homer, Buddhist Publishing Group, 1998.

Where the Buddha Trod: A Buddhist Pilgrimage, Major R. Raven-Hart, Lake House Investments Limited, Colombo, 1966.

Women & Buddhism, Spring Wind, Buddhist Cultural Forum, Vol. 6, No. 1, 2, & 3, 1986.

Woven Cadences of Early Buddhists (Sutta-Nipata), The Sacred Books of the Buddhists, Vol. XV, Trans. E.M. Hare, Oxford University Press, 1945.

Yasodhara, Newsletter on International Buddhist Women's Activities, Vol. 14, No. 2, January–March 1998.

Index